Fatherless Daughter

Emotionally Scared and Restricted

How to cope when you feel that you have been left behind.

SONYA H.

Contents

Acknowledgment

I Thank GOD first…second…and third. I want to thank each reader for allowing me to become a part of your journey and for purchasing this book.

Thank you to my family and friends for being so supportive as I let the world see me; I thank you for your love and trust.

I must also thank Pastor Chris Scott for encouraging me to become an author through our anthology (The Apple of his Eye); without that beginning, I might not have had the courage to put my life into words and for helping me with my spiritual growth.

Lastly, Thank you to my teacher Dr. Marita Kinney and her book writing classes. With her guidance, assurance, and confidence in me, I can write this book

and many more.

Foreword

BY PASTOR CHRIS SCOTT

The innermost joy of knowing that Life Coach, Missionary Sonya Hudson, has poured her heart into this powerful compilation of work has warmed my heart.

Sonya and I are connected by our Heavenly Father with love and admiration as my spiritual mentee. She has a heart of gold for others and is deeply committed to caring for their well-being. I am so proud and encouraged that she put this amazing literary work together, knowing that lives will be positively impacted, and her gift of encouragement with her illustrious nature will bring healing to many.

Sonya's journey through life will inspire you to look inside and enjoy the moments of peace, joy, and tranquility as she takes you through moments of treasured life experiences. The distinct presence in her life-changing stories is evident in her gracefulness and strength. Sonya's stories in this book will bring you to a place of euphoria, exhilaration, and enthusiasm. Sonya has a powerful warrior spirit, which shines through and leaps from the pages to touch the heart of the reader.

Sonya is truly one of God's favored daughters. She is a pleasure to have in my circle of true friends. She encourages and motivates all those she comes in contact with on a daily basis. I am glad that God laid it on the heart of Sonya to bless others with her intellectual ability to communicate love through her transparency.

I am sure each one of us has experienced days when we just need a word of encouragement sent by God. This book will bring about a level of encouragement and comfort. Sonya's strength and courage are evident in the words that transfer into the mind of the reader.

Well, my friend, missionary partner and Global Agent of Change has risen to the call to shine and share her intimate thoughts and experiences as she invites us to walk down memory lane through the streets of her mind. We are met with her vivacious spirit and beautiful melodies of life with optimism. Through her transparency, Sonya displays the fact that interruptions are opportunities to bring about change.

Knowing Sonya Hudson has impacted my life in a major way through the powerful tones of her inner being. As you read, be transformed by the emotional roller coaster of fear, faith, hope, truthfulness, confidence, resilience and joy flowing from a place of peace like a gentle breeze kissing your face on a midday in springtime!

Introduction

As you ride in this metaphorical car as a passenger in my early life's journey, be patient and understanding, and use it to demonstrate that everyone has a story. Everyone must decide how they will react to the challenges they face. The trials and tribulations, the learning and growing can be easier with help from a higher power. How you contend with your life's journey makes you, YOU.

My journey is how I traveled from Sonya Hill to Sonya Hudson. A name means a lot; it represents who you are. When a person talks to or about you, your name comes into play. How many times have you had to change your name? Do you know who you are? Are you the same person in your twenties that you are in your fifties?

Use the lines at the end of each chapter to note where you are right now, and as you move toward your destiny, you can see the change.

Thank you for traveling with me; I hope Fatherless Daughter helps you in yours

Chapter 1

Death

My father died a horrible death. He went out with his friends to celebrate. He got to intoxicated and was brought home by his friends who left him on the porch, but they didn't let anybody know he was there. He was too drunk; somehow, he choked on his vomit and died. His mother found him the next morning. This was a horrible experience for all involved, I'm sure his friend felt horrible their entire adult lives since they abandoned my dad when he should have been able to depend on them. That's the whole reason that you party with friends. My mother and father were friends from High School and started dating after they had graduated and he returned home after serving in the Army.

I was born to Sandra Webb and John Hill, Jr. in Schenectady, New York, where I lived until I was three. I am the oldest of two from my mother and my father's only child.

After my father passed away, his mother wanted my mother to allow her to raise me because she didn't have any girls, and I was her favorite son's only child. When my mother said no, my grandmother tried to pressure her, my mother continued to refuse her request so we weren't allowed to go to the funeral. My mother moved and never returned to New York and I never knew any of my dad's family.

My grandmother wanted a girl so badly that she took one of my cousins from her middle son and her mother and raised her; I think she agreed because she was young and pressured. I used to watch other kids with their dad, including my sister, and get so mad at God for taking mine. I was jealous of their relationships or what I believed their relationship was. In my head, my father was supposed to teach me so much, but I can't even remember what he looks like, smells like, or feels like, which makes me feel horrible. I would pray that God would give me a glimpse of him in a dream or something. But It never happened.

I used to feel so abandoned because my father passed away and left me. I was angry with God for taking him. Everyone else had their dads, and my mom told me that my dad loved me deeply. I felt abandoned even though my mother tried to love me enough for both; there is nothing like having a dad. At least, I would think.

I've so many mixed feelings about everything that has to do with my father. Why did we leave Schenectady and never go back? Why didn't my father's family look for me? Who are they? Where did I come from? I don't look like my mom, so do I look like my dad's family? I only have two pictures of my dad. How sad is that? I don't look like my mom at all: she has beautiful full lips, a more prominent nose, and is three inches shorter than me, which made things harder for me because I had no resemblance to her or anyone else in my family.

Let me tell you about my journey without my dad. My mother and I share a fatherless life. Her father was absent, although alive. He had a hard life, to say the least; he left home at 14 and began hustling to survive. He got my grandmother pregnant when he was only 19, and she was 18. What did he know about raising kids? Nothing, he had to hustle for everything he got, and he wasn't consistent in their lives.

I recently met four of my first cousins on my dad's side, thanks to my sister's diligent work searching for them. When my sister texted me with some information on my cousin, I had a complete meltdown in the shower crying for an hour until Ken came in and insisted that I get out; then he held me as I went to sleep. I think that all the emotions came to a head when my dream was finally coming true. They sent me several pictures before our meeting; they didn't know how important that was to me because now I can see where I came from. I look like the Hill family; my cousins welcomed and accepted me immediately, and the timing was perfect for us all.

My cousins went through their journey growing up, some good, some bad, as we all did, so when I wished I could have grown up with them, was God protecting me? How different would I have been? There is no way to know, but I believe so. I am glad I met them; my cousin Jamal and I look a lot alike, which makes me ecstatic.

FOOD FOR THOUGHT

Does how you live your life change your death? Does death change

a life?

_____

_____

_____

_____

_____

_____

_____

_____

_____

_____

_____

_____

_____

_____

_____

_____

_____

_____

_____

Chapter 2

WHO IS PROTECTING WHOM

We make decisions based on many things, and my family is no different. I thank God for every experience throughout my life and for allowing me to share some of them with you. I wouldn't change a thing. However, history can repeat itself unless we make changes; mom was fatherless, I was fatherless, and my daughters had a different type of fatherlessness.

My mother is a wonderful woman, very independent, and deeply religious in the Muslim faith. For my mom, marriage was necessary—a requirement within the religion; if one marriage didn't work, you married repeatedly until you got it right. She believed that children needed a father figure to help their growth and development. Could her father have done a better job even thou he was young? How different would she be?

My sister is almost three years younger than me, and she looked up to me more than I knew. My first stepfather lived with us in Springfield, Massachusetts. He was a wonderful man and brought along a wonderful family whom I love to this day. He was a light-skinned black man, over six feet tall, with broad shoulders and a deep voice, very handsome. We lived in a two-family flat with a basement; our house was the second house from the corner, and lucky for us, the bus stop was there. This house is the same place where I had my first fight. I was only eight years old, and a boy wanted to fight my sister because she disagreed with his little sister, and I wasn't having it. So I beat him up! Our sisters remained friends until we moved, but he and I never spoke again.

I remember when I was about six and my little sister was three, a friend of my mother lived with us during the week while she attended college. She was driving us to an outing in my mother's old blue Chevy when our car was struck by another vehicle at the intersection. My sister and I were crying, we had minor bumps and bruises, but our vehicle had a lot of damage. I was so scared. There weren't any cell phones back then, so I ran home, which wasn't too far, less than a mile. I was crying as I started stuttering because of my fear about the accident, so my mother had to be calm to help me relax enough to tell her what had happened. She knew there was a problem when I came home alone, but she contacted the authorities once I could explain what was happening. My mother expressed to me how proud she was of how I handled a serious situation. Although the car was totaled, there were no severe injuries.

FOOD FOR THOUGHT

Fight or Flight is a scientific response to fear, whether the fear is physical, emotional, or spiritual. What do you fear?

_____

_____

_____

_____

_____

_____

_____

_____

_____

_____

_____

_____

_____

_____

_____

_____

_____

Chapter 3

THE MOVE

When we moved from Massachusetts, it happened abruptly. My mother woke us up in the middle of the night, whispering, "Get up and move quickly and quietly," as she took us down to the basement of our two-story family flat with only trash bags carrying all our things. She put us into the car, and off we went. No warning. No conversation. Just off to a new life. This experience was traumatic for us as the friends we once knew were gone, and my stepfather didn't come with us. We never went back. At the time, we didn't know what was happening and when I asked my mom, she said, "Just go to sleep; it will all be okay." So, I did. Why we moved is my mother's story to tell.

When I woke, we had moved to Ypsilanti, Michigan. At this point, I was about nine years old, and my sister was six. We moved in with my aunt and cousins, who lived right down the street from my grandmother. That made the transition bearable, even though I didn't know them very well. They had moved there from Schenectady as well. My cousin and I became remarkably close, and I made good friends. Life began to get back to normal. Shortly after we moved there, we got a "green" three-bedroom townhouse with a basement in the same apartment complex, which was exciting because I started feeling more secure with where we lived.

Sometime later, my stepfather arrived, and our family thrived. I was enjoying my life again. I loved living there.

I had my first peck on the lips when I was twelve by this super cute guy as we sat on my front porch. I had a few more fights, none of which I started, and experienced death for the first time when my favorite great-uncle died of pneumonia. I was the last to see him alive; we were at my grandmother's house, where he lived, just talking about life as we usually did when I asked him to go to the hospital for them to check on his breathing. He refused and said if he didn't feel better tomorrow, he would go to the doctor and see what was wrong. I knew he wasn't doing very well, but nobody took me seriously because he downplayed his sickness. He died the next day. His death hurt me so much. My grandmother, his sister, couldn't go back into her house as he died sitting at her kitchen table. She was out of town at her mother's funeral when he died, and when she returned, she moved into a high-rise for seniors. My grandmother was also upset because my great-uncle was buried with her dentures in his mouth, so she had to buy new ones. Even with all this going on, I was there with my family and friends, so life was great.

My stepfather was good to my sister and I, but what we didn't know is that he wasn't always good to my mother. The first time I saw them fighting, my stepfather had my mom pinned down, partially on the bed, with her feet hanging, barely touching the floor. She was yelling and struggling to get up. I couldn't understand why he was holding her down. When I yelled at him, he looked at me, which allowed her to grab the telephone on the headboard behind her, and she hit him in the head. He told me to go to my room, and my mom was able to get away from him. I was so scared that I could hardly breathe. My heart was pounding, I was crying, and all I could do was lie in my bed and rock until I fell asleep. Sometime later, my mom made him move out, which made me sad, too, because he was the only father I knew, and I loved him and his whole family. He never said goodbye. I never saw him again. He abandoned me. Two fathers were gone. My sister started looking up to me, and I became the family's protector. At least, I thought that was my job.

God is the true protector, keep him the head of your life.

FOOD FOR THOUGHT

Even though my mother raised my sister and me with love, security, and courage, why did I feel that we needed protection? Whose is your protector?

_____

_____

_____

_____

_____

_____

_____

_____

_____

_____

_____

_____

_____

_____

_____

_____

_____

_____

Chapter 4

ALL HELL BREAKS LOSE

We continued to live in the green townhouses, and it was time for me to start middle school. I was so excited to join my cousin at the local middle school where all of our friends went, but my mom had different plans. She decided that we needed to move to Inkster, Michigan, about 30 minutes from where we were living, and we had to change schools from public schools to private Muslim schools. This was a shock. No warning, no conversation, just another traumatic move, leaving family and friends behind.

I didn't know anyone in my new neighborhood. This school was completely different; we didn't ride on the yellow bus to school; a white van would pick us up in front of the house and take us to Detroit for school. The van ride was about twenty minutes if we went directly there, but we had to pick up other kids, so it took about an hour each way. The mandatory uniform for the females was; a long oversized green skirt that touched the ground, with a long oversized sleeveless green top that stopped close to our knees, a white long-sleeved shirt under our top, and a scarf that covered our heads. We wore this uniform no matter what the season. I was so embarrassed about wearing the uniform even though I didn't have any friends in the neighborhood. I didn't want anyone outside school to see me; I hated being different. I hated for people to stare at me, so I would wear a pair of jeans under my skirt so that I could pull my uniform skirt up and put it all under a jacket so that the only thing that was showing was my jeans and jacket, with a hood or hat so that you wouldn't know I was wearing a scarf. I didn't believe in what the Muslim culture represented and what they taught, nor did I agree with their treatment of women. I later realized that every Muslim wasn't that way. I am thankful that after this experience my mother gave me the choice and I chose Christianity. My mother was born and raised as a Christian. Her mother didn't really attend church, but her grandmother did and would take her regularly as a child. My mother had a negative experience with the church and decided to become a Muslim when I was about three years old as she moved us to Massachusetts.

My school didn't look like a regular school. It was a small, two-story building with classrooms on both levels, with a large open room for praying and gathering when they wanted everyone together. When I started my new school, I was angry and depressed, even though I had made a few friends. I was insulting, disrespectful, mean, argumentative, and aggressive to every person of authority. I was in so much pain and didn't know what to do with it, so I adopted the "I didn't care" attitude which was very unhealthy. I no longer wanted to live after so many abrupt moves and too much change. I couldn't bear it anymore, so I took a bottle of pills, believing it would be over soon. Only it wasn't. I woke up madder than I was the night before. What happened? How was I alive? Why didn't God want me? He left me alone to stay here and suffer. My third father was gone. I thought Jesus Christ didn't want to be bothered with me, either. I recalled my father's death as he had left me in the world, alone with no protection. My stepfather followed suit and now God. The resources of today weren't as readily available as they are now, nor was the topic discussed as openly as it is today and we still have attempted suicide and suicide. This is real, pain can be so overwhelming that you can't see the light at the end of the tunnel.

My behavior became worse. No one could tell me what to do and when they would try, I would do the opposite. I was a complete hot mess.

My mother never knew that I was that depressed. I don't think it would have resulted in me changing schools, but she would have tried to comfort and talk me through being in that place, which wouldn't have helped me at all. Only one friend knew I had taken the pills, and she was scared until she saw me at school the next day.

I'm not sure why none of the teachers told my mother about my behavior. She wouldn't have tolerated it. They thought it was a temporary situation and I would grow out of it. It didn't happen that year, and during the summer, we had to go to a Muslim camp which I hated; However, it was only for a week, but I still hated the fact that I had to be around these people during my summer vacation. I planned to return to Ypsilanti to stay with my cousins and grandmother. I don't remember whose idea it was. But a few girls, including me, decided that we didn't like this one girl, so we were going to make it look like she had urinated on herself during the night. One of the girls urinated in a coke can, and another girl poured it on her and the bed, but she woke up and saw us standing there and told on us. I was the only one that got into trouble. The camp counselor said I had to have been the ringleader even though I didn't pee in the can nor pour the pee on her. So, I had to write an apology letter to her and read it to the entire camp, admitting guilt. You would think I would have been embarrassed, but I wasn't; I didn't even care.

I was a leader at an early age; I was the ring leader in this unfortunate situation. I didn't know that there were good and bad leaders, and I was leading people in the wrong direction.

In the Eighth Grade, I got into trouble in school but not as much as in the Seventh Grade. I calmed down some until closer to the end of the school year when the principal decided he would punish me for unruly behavior. Usually, the staff would have the entire school enter the praying hall, and they would paddle you in front of everyone. They did that often— it didn't matter if you were a boy or girl, a man would have you bend over the chair in the front of the auditorium and paddle you; of course, they would cry and be embarrassed in front of everyone, but that was the point. He knew that wouldn't fly with me, so he took a different approach. He told me to go and sit in the Fourth-Grade classroom to do my classwork, thinking this punishment would embarrass me into behaving. I wasn't embarrassed, but I was tired of fighting the world. So, I did as I was told and went to the classroom, completed the work, and attempted to turn the work in the following day to the principal.

When I arrived at school the next day, I followed the principal's instructions and brought my homework to his office to be checked so I could return to my classroom. The assistant principal was there, but the principal was not. I showed my work to the assistant principal, who told me I could return to my class. About an hour later, the principal realized I was back in my regular class. He came to my class and tried to embarrass me again, instructing me to return to the Fourth-Grade class, but I refused. I refused because, although I did what I was told, he wanted to continue to punish me unnecessarily. The staff took pride in embarrassing kids. They thought this would motivate us not to misbehave, but it didn't work for me. As we argued about returning to the Fourth-Grade class, he wouldn't allow me to call my mother, so the secretary snuck out and called her. He was screaming at me, threatening me, and I was doing the same to him. My mother could hear the commotion over the phone and rushed to the school to find complete chaos.

My mother arrived and followed the principal around the school, trying to find out what was going on, and he kept ignoring her and walking off while she was talking. Muslim women didn't have a voice, especially divorced women with two kids, and could not question the principal's authority. He went into the boy's bathroom to avoid her, thinking she wouldn't follow him, but she did. The fear of a man hitting my mother surfaced again, so in order to protect her, I retrieved a knife from a friend at school and went into the bathroom where they were with the full intent of stabbing him. I started threatening the principal with the knife, which shocked my mother because no one had ever told her about my behavior. She had always thought that I was an excellent, well-behaved child, as I was at home. I was expelled that day, and my mother also removed my sister. I was free, but I had to go through another change. I thought we would move back to Ypsilanti, where I would go to school with my cousins, but that was not the case. My mother had other plans; she always tried to do what was best for us, so we moved to another city Michigan and started going to Romulus Middle School with only a month left. She took us to school every day until she found an apartment, and we moved again. Starting a new school was a little stressful, but I was relieved to be out of the Muslim school. I had never been to Romulus before, and we didn't know anybody there. We started in a two-bedroom apartment until a three-bedroom became available. Living in Romulus was great. I went to high school, played basketball and ran track, I met an amazing boy who I experienced my first love with, he too was a popular athlete with the most amazing green eyes, we spent as much time as we possibly could as we shared the same friends—of course, I got into a fight—but everything was beautiful until my mother remarried a man with two boys younger than us. Then it happened again. We moved away. We moved to St. Louis, Missouri; my new stepfather's job transferred him, so off we went. I begged my mom to let me live with my grandmother, but she said no, that I was her responsibility and she would be the one to raise me. Sad, once again, because of another move. My mom allowed me to stay in Michigan over the summer with my best friend (at the time) and her family until school started, and then I had to go to Missouri. That was the best summer ever because I had more time with my first love and my best friend. There is always some good to be found, even in bad situations.

Life in Missouri for the first six months was tough. Back then, we had to pay for long-distance calls so we could only call every other weekend for only a few moments, so my first Love and I would write letters, and I would sign them with perfume and a kiss using some of my mother's lipstick. Eventually, we faded out.

FOOD FOR THOUGHT

How we treat and teach children is how we mold the world's future.

How can you better mold the future?

Chapter 5

THE BEATING TO THE CORPS

My new high school was in a well to do diverse area, I joined the basketball team after months of being sad and eating lunch by myself, basketball made it easier for me to make friends. St. Louis wasn't a bad place to live. I went to a good school and lived in a lovely house, but things started to change when my stepfather became abusive to my mother.

One day I walked in on my stepfather straddling my mother as she laid on the floor in the living room. He held her down with her hands above her head as she struggled to get up, calling for help. I launched into attack mode and started swinging on him till he got off her, and then I ran out of the house across the street and up the long driveway to my girlfriend's house and stayed there. My heart was racing and I was breathing and sweating extremely hard, I thought he was following me. But, on some level I felt like I was my mother's super hero. My job was to protect her. When I talked to my mother, she told me to stay there until everything cooled off, which was only for the rest of the day. When I looked outside, I saw that he had thrown all my things on the front porch and in the yard for everyone to see, but before I went home, my mother took everything and put it back in my room. He wanted me out of the house but my mother wasn't allowing that. Plus, I wouldn't have left my sister.

I had the entire basement to myself. My bedroom, a connecting bathroom, the laundry room, and a vast living room with glass doors opened to a fenced-in backyard where we had a dog named Bullet. I loved it.

My stepfather might have been trying to do the right thing when he tried to give my sister a whooping; he had her pent to the dining room wall with one hand and hit her with the belt with the other hand. Whipping my sister didn't sit well with me. She screamed as you do when you're being hit with a belt; I attacked. I swung at him, hit him, grabbed the belt, and beat him with it. Then, I ran and called my mother from my same friend's house. My mother told me to stay over there until she got home from work, and she'd deal with it then.

Each time, my mother would smooth everything over with everybody, and we would move forward. Remember that I always felt like I had to be the family's protector and would do just that. That feeling of being the protector didn't change just because I had a new stepfather.

I wasn't a perfect child like my mom thought, but I was very loving and respectful to most people. I wasn't disrespectful in any other school except for the Muslim school, even though I used to fight a lot, especially in Michigan.

One night, I was in my room in the basement when I was awakened by banging and yelling upstairs. My heart started pounding, fear kicked in again, and it sounded worse than any other incident. I ran up the ten stairs to find my mother and stepfather arguing and tussling. As she went out the door into the garage to get in my gray Ford Fusion to get away from him, he followed her, grabbed a baseball bat sitting by the carport door, and busted out the driver's side window as she tried to flee. I ran to the kitchen drawer. He saw me through the glass door and came after me, my mother coming behind him. I grabbed the largest butcher knife I could find in those quick moments and turned toward him, yelling as I threatened to kill him. Time seemed like it was moving so slowly, yet everything happened at warp speed. I genuinely wanted to kill him and would have if a big burly white police officer hadn't come in the door. The officer observed me threatening my stepfather and told me to put the knife down in an extremely calm voice. He didn't have his weapon drawn, which he would have every right to do for his safety and the safety of the rest of my family. I told him I couldn't put the knife down because I had to kill him. The police officer guaranteed that if I put the knife down, he would take care of the situation for me. My mom begged me to put the knife down. As I put it down, my stepfather ran through the house out the front door, jumped in his station wagon, and sped off up the street. The police officer chased him on foot and then by car until he was caught and arrested.

That was a pivotal moment in my life. I shared the race of the officer to show that all white officers are not bad. At that point, I decided that I wanted to be a cop. And that I wanted to be the protector of those suffering, especially from domestic violence. Once I became a police officer I truly understood how that officer decision not to arrest me and to only focus on my stepfather changed the trajectory of my life. My step father wasn't allowed back at the house and they later divorced.

I graduated high school and returned to Michigan that summer until I left to join the Marine Corps. Many people asked why I chose the Marine Corps, and I told them the Marine Corps chose me. While at the mall one Saturday afternoon, I noticed a black female and male walking around in uniform. I wanted to do whatever the two of them did because they looked fantastic in their uniforms. They exuded success. I approached them and inquired; they happened to be Marine Corps recruiters. They came to the house to talk to my mom, and even though she was surprised that I wanted to join, she agreed. I called my cousin, who was still in Michigan and asked her to join me, she agreed, and we both joined on October 27, 1986.

Imagine two black females joining a white male dominant workforce. The Marine Corps was demanding; I remember when my journey began; I was at the airport waiting to fly to Paris Island, South Carolina, where female marines had training (boot camp). While waiting, I was chewing my gum, popping, of course, when a male staff sergeant ran up to me, cussing and fussing about my chewing gum, he scared me so bad that I swallowed my gum by accident. Our flight was scheduled to land at night, so when we took the bus to the base, it would be extremely late, and we would be tired, so we wouldn't recognize the direction in which we came. Most people were sleeping on the bus when we arrived since we had been driving for so long, so when the male drill instructor quietly came on the bus and began screaming at the top of his lungs for us to get off the bus, he scared us all. I was thinking, what am I doing here? My cousin wasn't on this bus with me because she was flying out of Michigan, and I was coming from Missouri. As we were all corralled into the squad bay, our new female drill instructors talked to us for hours, and we were paying close attention. Have you noticed that there hasn't been a bathroom break? Correct, and we were all too scared to ask. One girl had to go so badly that she urinated on the floor. The drill instructor went crazy on her through words and in her face. She cried as she cleaned it up, and we moved on.

The military is very strategic in what they do; everything is to prepare you for a possible mission. For example; we had to repel off of a building; this was the hardest thing for me because I am afraid of heights, my drill instructor kept yelling at me as she got closer and closer in my face, which pushed me back closer to the edge to eventually I had no choice but to repel. I screamed the entire way down but I used what she taught me to stop myself before I got to the ground. The Marine Corps and organizations like it often work on you mentally to control you physically, and it works so well; I graduated from Marine Corps boot camp January 1987 knowing I was all that and a bag of chips. I learned so much from my experiences in the Corps.

FOOD FOR THOUGHT

You never know what happens in a person's house. It doesn't matter the size of the house. What house did you grow up in?

_____

_____

_____

_____

_____

_____

_____

_____

_____

_____

_____

_____

_____

_____

_____

_____

_____

_____

_____

Chapter 6

CAN YOU CRY

I know God had my back even when I didn't believe He did. Every aspect of my life was important as it made me who I am. Every experience, good and bad, was a part of my journey. We think clichés like "after heartache comes ease" doesn't mean anything, but they are right. Most sayings come from people who have experienced something significant and made it through. I also had a praying mother. No matter her religion, mom believed in God and instilled in me that He was always sitting next to me. When times are hard, it is difficult to feel God's presence. Knowing can be enough.

For me crying was a sign of weakness; maybe if I had allowed myself to cry, I would have been less emotionally restricted. When I needed to cry, I would give myself a certain amount of time, such as ten minutes; I would time myself, and let loose for only that amount of time, then shut it off, and I didn't allow myself to cry about that issue again. My mom and sister always cried, so she didn't teach this behavior. For me, this was the only way I could be the protector of my family. How unhealthy! Now I have all these emotions boxed up, sitting on the shelf in my heart with nowhere to go. I fear opening these boxes because I don't know what will come out. Am I over my past?

God made me tough to prepare me for another level in life. My childhood was good—I had some challenging times—but I emphasized the good times more than the bad.

My mom focused on ensuring that she provided a safe, secure, and loving environment for her girls, and she did just that. I'm proud that my mother didn't keep us in an abusive situation. She left the relationship to protect herself and us when things turned sour. She was always very affectionate and made decisions based on our needs. If she had financial struggles, we didn't know about it. I never had to worry about if we had enough food to eat. I didn't know that I grew up poor until my mother and I were talking while I was in my fifties and she explained her struggles to me.

Like so many of us, my mother had terrible taste in men. In her defense, her father and grandfather were not good role models.

My experiences with the Muslim religion were negative, so I started reading the Bible to understand

Christ better. I'm still growing in my walk with God, and I pray that he continues to guide my steps.

Looking back at my life, I realize that God has been with me all along, even when I was mad at him. God never said that we wouldn't go through anything; he said that he would be there with us. God is always sitting next to us. Treat Him like he's your best friend. Talk to Him and listen to Him. You are not alone. Be the change agent in your life. Be blessed. You are so loved.

No one has a perfect childhood. Parenting is a trial-and-error experiment; each child is different, and each experience is perceived differently. How you deal with hardship is what separates you from others. It hasn'talways been easy, but if you look at life like everything comes down to how you choose to react to harsh conditions, it can change your life forever. For example, decide not to get upset with something as small as when someone cuts you off while driving. Allow them grace, send them blessings, and see how it makes you feel. It has made a substantial difference in my life. I don't do it all the time as I should, but I am a work in progress.

Growing up, even though my childhood was a roller-coaster ride, life wasn't always great. Sometimes I felt like life was pretty F****D up. However, studies have shown that people react to situations by one of three actions; fight, flight or freeze. I have learned how to master living life in fight or flight mode, by quickly assessing a situation and reacting. I can talk, listen or fight my way through anything. And fighting is not always physical. This talent has helped me in my career choices as an adult. I fulfilled my dream of becoming a police officer and served my community for over 25 years. I worked my way through the ranks from officer through assistant chief at a what started out as a white male dominate police department in the Atlanta area. There were many challenges from within the department and with the community but it was the best choice that I could have made for my life. Through the talents that God has blessed me with I was able to help many people which fills my heart with Joy.

FOOD FOR THOUGHT

Is crying a sign of weakness, or does it help to free you by clearing the soul?

_____

_____

_____

_____

_____

_____

_____

_____

_____

_____

_____

_____

_____

_____

_____

_____

_____

Chapter 7

A BOY

When your father is missing in action for whatever reason, it affects all your decisions, especially my relationships with men, so I looked for love in all the wrong places. I'm only going to speak about one boyfriend even though I had many. He wasn't my first or last boyfriend, he had a powerful impact on my life. I was in my early twenties and smitten with him from the first moment I saw him. He looked like Malcolm X, and I thought he was gorgeous. I thought we were meant to be together forever because that's the pitch he gave. That was not the case. Or maybe it was the case for that season. During that season, he taught me how NOT to love myself. He made me feel as if my body was ugly. Even though my mom told me I was beautiful my whole life and as years passed, other men would say how beautiful I was; I could never get past the fact that he thought I wasn't beautiful...Is what a man thinks of you more important than what you feel about yourself? You might be saying to yourself, "Oh, that wouldn't happen to me; I'm too confident" Well, it can happen to you. Words are powerful and cannot be unsaid. He mistreated me in several ways on many occasions, but I kept coming back for more. My experience with this man lowered my self-esteem and caused me to have numerous superficial relationships. I stopped believing that I was worthy of the best. I was always searching for something. He ultimately left me heartbroken and vulnerable for the next man.

He undermined my confidence in personal relationships and my femininity, which hindered my relationships so much that when things felt a little rocky, I would run as fast as I could with no thought to the person I was leaving. I was exceptional at pretending to be confident.

Fatherlessness impacts every aspect of your life, even if your father is in the house but not engaged in your life. His father never taught him how to treat and love women.

Now that I'm in my fifties, I have changed the way I see myself, the way I see others, and the way that I love. It's the weirdest thing. Don't waste all the time that I did.

FOOD FOR THOUGHT

Why is it that the negative stuff impacts our lives so much more than the positive? Why does trauma stay with us longer than good experiences?

_____

_____

_____

_____

_____

_____

_____

_____

_____

_____

_____

_____

_____

_____

_____

_____

_____

Chapter 8

IS TWO REALLY BETTER THAN ONE
(the words of my daughter Tamika Bradley)

I am writing about my experience with a faraway bio (biological) father and a close-up stepfather. I was born from a pure accident during a one-time lust-filled weekend of fun. That said, my mom and bio dad was never meant to be together, so here we are with a single mother doing everything she can to make it work. My mom always said, God don't make any mistakes. I did have a small relationship with my bio dad because of my mom, of course. She would ensure that there were phone conversations, gifts on essential days (Birthday, Christmas), and the oh-so "fun" but mandatory summer visits. I wasn't fond of visiting my bio dad during the summers. I had my own life, friends, and activities at home, so visiting was something I did to appease my mother and because I didn't have a choice. Not every trip was terrible, but not every trip was good.

It's crazy how you remember more bad times than the good ones, though I think that's with anything. I remember my bio dad had a girlfriend (now his widow), and she brought two kids (a son and a daughter) into the relationship; needless to say, we did not get along. I remember a particular incident when her son (my step-brother) kicked me in the eye (on purpose) while we played outside. I bent down to fix the chain on my bike, and he was playing around and kicking his feet. I had asked him to stop (maybe not in a nice manner), and he kicked me in the face. I was bleeding and crying, and when I went to tell the adults, I was told by my bio dad that I should have defended myself and that I should not be crying. He got yelled at, but that was the just of his punishment. I definitely felt like he needed a harsher punishment, like a nice ass whooping.

I never fully felt that I fit in with them; I always felt like the outcast, the kid that only came around every so often to try and ensure that Hertis (bio dad) didn't look like a complete deadbeat dad. Since he never came to visit me while I was living with my mother and child support was pretty much nonexistent, that factious façade didn't hold up for long. I had a bit of support from my paternal grandmother, who lived close by and made me feel loved and not like a complete outsider, but she passed away a couple of years before I stopped visiting. I believe my bio dad loved me in his own way.

I remember an incident with my stepmother that I will never forget. I decided to cook for the family to show some love because cooking is what I love to do; I made tacos for everyone, and for whatever reason that I have never found out, she told her children not to eat my food. Imagine being an eleven-year-old girl trying to figure out where she fits in; how do you think she handled that rejection? Well, not great, but the only thing I could do was cry and share my tacos with my grandmother. I can't fully explain how that made me feel because I never really understood why she didn't like me. I won't downplay the difficulty of being a step-parent, but you have to understand what you sign up for when you get with someone that already has children. It's interesting how a grown woman can have so much dislike for a child. I say that because she wasn't the only grown woman that didn't like me. Crazy right? Well, the only person (at the time) that shared a biological connection with me through my father was my big sister, and her mother didn't really care about me either.

I can remember a time when my sister and I were at my bio dad's house, and it was time for her to go back home with her mother. I was very sad because we were close, and I felt like she was the only one who really loved me. I asked her mother if I could go with them and spend the night at their house. She told me not today because they had something to do, but I could come over on a different day. When that day came, I was so excited; I had all kinds of plans and fun stuff for us to do when I got over there. I packed my bag and waited on the front porch for GOD knows how long, and she never showed up. I never found out what excuse she gave for not coming to get me that day, but after all that, I never wanted to go back to visit, and my mother never made me again. I later found out why she wasn't too fond of me.

It turns out my father lied to my mom; he was married to my sister's mother and had an affair with my mother, and accidentally got her pregnant. Can you guess who popped out of her lady parts, ME! That's right; she hated me because I was the product of an affair that ruined her marriage. I don't blame her for being upset; we are all human beings and can't always control our feelings and emotions.

In 2018 while on a TDY (temporary duty assignment) in Ohio, which was only a few hours from where my bio dad lived, I found out that he was sick, so I made it a priority to see him again. Prior to that, I hadn't been around that side of my family for well over ten years, But I felt it was important to see him and for my only son to meet his grandfather, I knew this might be the only chance we would have since his health was declining. It was interesting how all those old emotions and feelings resurfaced the moment I got to their house. All the hurt and feeling of not being enough to truly be a part of the family was still there. I remember going into his room to see him and sitting on the bed next to him and my stepmother; she began trying to apologize and make amends, but I didn't feel that it was genuine. I smiled and accepted her apology even though I felt she was doing it because she knew that it would make him happy on his deathbed, and I knew how important his happiness was to her. It's crazy how one can hold on to pain and hurt for so long. I am speaking for myself as well.

My bio father passed from Multiple Myeloma and Amyloidosis in March of 2019. I have to admit; I do feel like my step mother genuinely loved him. I loved my bio father too, very much, but I realized that he was unable to protect me emotionally, and that seems to be a thing for men in general. My relationship with my bio dad was nonexistent until I discovered he was dying. I know that might sound harsh, but it's reality. By Webster's definition, being a father and being a dad is one in the same, or the term can be interchangeable, but I disagree. I feel that anyone can be a father, but not everyone can be a dad. Fathering children is when you get someone pregnant after having sex. Being a dad is being emotionally present in someone's life and physically being present to assist in raising said child. That brings me to my step-dad, who came into my life when I was about 10.

He stepped up to the plate, raised me, and adopted my sister, he wanted to adopt me, but my bio dad wouldn't let him. My step-dad was the dad my sister and I were missing; He taught us how to drive and he threatened many a boyfriend in our dating lives. He walked us down the aisle at our weddings ten years apart. I feel he was there when I needed a present father in my life and I am incredibly grateful for that. I had to realize that despite all of the great things he did in my life as a child it doesn't make him perfect. I had him on a pedestal, so when he made a mistake (a huge mistake), it was a hard pill to swallow. Being faithful to one partner seems challenging for many men, but I thought it would come easy to my stepfather (being on that pedestal and all). I was wrong!

It's interesting being the eldest child and dealing with a situation like this. I never fully grieved over the breakup of my parents because I didn't feel as though I was allowed to show my emotions. I remember being told that my younger siblings were watching me and for me to watch my reaction due to the possibility of distorting my siblings' vision of our father. I feel he didn't just owe my mother an apology; he also owed his children one. He needs to understand that he broke up our family and caused pain in all of us, not just her. To me, it was selfish on his part to mess up the family, then move on to another family so quickly. I have never really spoken about my feelings because I wanted to protect the image of my step-dad for my sister and brother.

It was easier for me because I was much older than my siblings; I was married and no longer lived in the same household. It took a toll on me a lot later in my life and with my marriage. Since the demise of my marriage, I haven't had much luck in the dating world. I'm unsure if it has anything to do with the trust issues I have with men or my lack of faith in marriage. I think the anger and disapproval come when I realized that he made a conscious decision to step outside the marriage. As a grown man, you knew that stepping out would ruin your family, and you chose to do it anyway. Not just once; oh no, once would have been a mistake, but multiple times. People (men more than women) don't think about who is affected by their decisions; they just think about themselves at that moment. He didn't consider or care about how his daughters would react, think, or even feel. He didn't think about the example he set for his sons on how to treat women.

Well, that is neither here nor there because everyone has "moved on." He has remarried, and so has my mother. It was difficult meeting the new woman in his life since it was so soon after the divorce. I don't remember meeting her before they married, which was another issue I had. I will never forget when my little sister called me on the phone and told me to check my stepfather's Facebook page. As soon as I clicked on his name, the first thing that popped up was a photo of a female hand with a diamond ring on her finger, and the caption was, "She said yes!".

The sadness, behind the anger, in my sister's voice, was heartbreaking. I had no idea what I was supposed to say as the big sister, so I just let her vent and tried to cover for him as usual. My step-dad is still very active in my life, and I am thankful for that.

Having two father figures was indeed a blessing. My story may have come off a little harsh, but it was just my truth. I love both of my dad's, flaws and all. I have learned a lot about myself, relationships, and life. The tribulations allowed my mother an opportunity to teach us what a strong, successful black woman looks like with and without a husband; I am indebted to her for that.

I was always told that GOD would never put more on your plate than you could handle; I think that it is safe to assume that he knew I would need two dads to make me the woman that I am today. So, to answer my question, YES, two dads were definitely better than one!

FOOD FOR THOUGHT

Can a stepfather bring as much value to your life as a biological father?

_____

_____

_____

_____

_____

_____

_____

_____

_____

_____

_____

_____

_____

_____

_____

_____

_____

Chapter 9

THE STEPPED UP FATHER
(the words of my daughter, Tamia Green)

The definition of a father; is a man in relation to his child or children. The definition of a dad, funny enough, is one's father. It is kind of weird to think that all you must do is, be a man in relation to a child, and you get to be called a father.

Well, for me, that is not the case. In my world, being a man in relation to a child is called a sperm donor, which I have. Don't feel bad for me, though, because I also have a father. Let's dig into the story of what I thought happened and what actually happened. My life for the first 16 years seemed as normal as can be. I grew up in a happy and loving two-parent household until I was about eleven or twelve when my dad's wondering penis got the best of him, and my parents separated. Before the separation, my dad and I were really cool. I always liked to think I was and still am his favorite child. My dad did work a lot, so he did not have much free time for us, but when he did, I remember we would go fishing together and eat wings in his man-cave. I have always been a momma's girl, but I did love my daddy; he would do anything for me. During the separation, I did not know the exact reason my parents were divorcing. Honestly, I was glad I didn't know. If I had known how my father hurt my mother at that time, we probably would've had a different relationship. Still, since I was unaware, I was just sad to see my dad go. I have always held my mom up on a pedal stool, so I knew she was not in the wrong and that it had to be for a good reason, but I was content leaving that situation up to the parents. My mom has always protected us from the information she felt we couldn't handle back then, and my mom always knows best. She has always protected my feelings as best she can and has always promoted a close and healthy relationship with my dad. She always pushes this relationship because she missed out on a relationship with her dad as he died when she was three years old. At the current age of fifty-four, I still don't believe that void has ever been filled for her.

Back to my dad, after my parents separated, my dad took it very hard; as he should, my mother is the best he'll ever get. With him taking it so hard, he started spiraling downhill. His behavior changed which made it difficult to spend time with him. I remember he only lived three minutes away from us, and my brother and I had to go over there at least every other weekend. Still, we weren't restricted to those days only. I hated going over there because he had some unhealthy relationships with a plethora of women that weren't always favorable for us as his children.

All I felt was anger; the sadness was not yet present. I used to be so mad because, before the separation, we saw my dad every day. Now that we don't see him nearly as often, you would think he would want to spend this time wisely with his children, but he did not. Eventually, I got fed up and told him that if he did not stop his unruly behavior, I would stop coming to see him. Surprisingly, nothing changed, so I stopped seeing him for a few months. Of course, my mom was putting in more work than him, trying to convince me to go back over there because she values my relationship with my dad, but I wasn't feeling like he was acting like the dad he used to be. I have always been more about action than a title.

Eventually, I started going back over there. Still, I wasn't too happy about it, and I honestly don't think, to this day, our relationship has ever fully healed. I understand that my dad is human, and that was the only way he could cope at the time, but it made me lose a lot of trust in him. It made me see him as weak, unreliable, and untrustworthy.

I was 16 years old, and my mom and I were lying in her bed watching Law and Order: SVU. One of the injured young ladies was in the hospital, and her parent came to do a blood transfusion. In doing this, she discovered that her parent was not biologically related to her, meaning they could not give blood. This was a shock for her. I then turned to my mom, not thinking anything of it, and being nonchalant, I said, "What if y'all weren't my parents?". In saying this, I chuckled and was ready to move on, but my mom looked at me and said,

"What if we weren't?". I laughed; I did not take her seriously because if anyone knows us, they know that my mom and I look just alike, she couldn't say I wasn't hers if she wanted to, and that's what my response was. She then paused the TV, and at this point, my heart started beating faster, and confusion was taking over my body. What was she about to say? I could tell she wasn't joking, so I was scared. She then proceeded to explain to me that my dad was not my biological father. At that point, I couldn't hear anything else she was saying; I felt like I was going to have an anxiety attack; what was she even talking about, and why was she doing this? I remember trying to act normal because I never want to hurt my mom's feelings. Growing up, we never really cried or showed emotions other than happy or mad, so I was trying to fight back the tears. I remember telling myself, "What the hell do you want to cry for? Just make it to your room.".. I remember asking a few questions about my bio-father but not many because I couldn't think that hard. I then told her I needed a minute and went to my room.

I remember getting to my room, and my thoughts ran crazy as the room spun. I sat down and started thinking, how could someone leave their daughter, how could someone not wonder about their daughter, how could someone be so f$%^&*g selfish? What did I do so wrong at that young age to deserve this? How could he not love me, and how can I move on knowing this? My dad was an amazing man for taking in a child that was not his and raising her as his own; it made me feel that much more loved by him. Then I thought, how could my mom lie to me like this for all these years? I thought I could trust her; what else was she lying about? Who else knows this? My whole family is full of liars. After a lot more thinking, a little bit of crying, and so much confusion, I went back to my mom with questions. All the questions came out, one or two at a time, with days and even weeks in between, but I wanted to know who he was, if she had pictures and if I had any other siblings who knew about me. I wanted to know the whole story.

The whole story was this: my mom dated my biological father for a short period of time and ended up pregnant. After finding out she was pregnant, she discovered that he was trying to return to his wife after being separated for about a year. Of course, she was heartbroken in the very beginning that they weren't going to be together, but she still allowed him to be a part of my life. As I said before, my mom is a very sweet woman. Anyway, my biological father was in the marines and was being transferred to California. My mom would not allow her infant to fly to California and he wasn't going to come to see me so the relationship faltered.

My mom and adopted dad started dating when I was almost a year old, married when I was three, and dad adopted me when I was four. After very little convincing, my biological father willingly signed over all his parental rights and agreed not to have any contact with me until I was at least 18 years old. Without hesitation, they went to file the paperwork, and I became a Porter.

During my mother and I's many different conversations, it was disclosed that I had three older brothers, two of which lived within thirty minutes of my house. A few weeks after all this information came out, my adopted dad came by the house to see us, and my mom yelled out, "she knows about her biological father." The following two minutes went by in slow motion. My dad and I sat on the couch, and my mom stood up. I could hear my dad's heart beating so hard and fast; he slowly looked up at my mom and then turned and looked at me.

The moment was awkward; I remember my dad saying, "I thought we weren't going to tell her yet and that we were going to tell her together." My mom then explained that it wasn't planned; she just felt that particular moment was the right moment. Quickly following that, my dad turned to talk to me; I still do not know to this day what he said or what I said at that moment. It was intense and brutal to get through.

Life continued, and everything was pretty smooth; of course, it was still in the back of my mind, but I could occupy my time where the thoughts did not take over. Fast forward to right before my 18th birthday, when my biological father's ex-wife, the mother of 2 of my three brothers from him, decided she wanted to find me. This phenomenal woman searched high and low to find my mom. Mind you, my mom was not a social media person at the time, so she was not easy to find, but this woman did not let that stop her; she found out where my mom worked and made some phone calls which eventually got her in contact with my mom. She said she knew my 18th birthday was quickly approaching, and she wanted me to be able to meet my brothers. My mom was shocked but quickly spoke to me about it; I was very nervous, but my curiosity would not let me turn that opportunity down. My mom and I went to Buffalo Wild Wings on March 21, 2016, and I met two of my brothers and their mother. As we walked in to meet them, my palms were sweating, and my heart was racing, but I knew I had my mom by my side and could accomplish anything with her. We went in there, and my big 6 foot plus brothers, towering over my petite 5'4 behind, I must admit it was a little intimidating. Still, they were so excited and sweet, which warmed my heart. They were huggers, which at first was a little weird, but I am a hugger too, so I got over it quickly.

I remember we sat there for a few hours and got to know one another. They are only a few years older than me and only lived about thirty minutes down the road from me; how weird is that? It was crazy to me how fast I connected with my brothers and how close we still are to this day, and those two as well as their mom are the best thing that came out of this entire situation, hands down. Only days after meeting my brothers, my biological father found out and decided to come down from California for my brother's 21st birthday. He wanted to meet me, and of course, curiosity took over again, and I dragged my mom along as we celebrated my brother at the "Main Event" in Atlanta. I met my biological father, along with many other family members, for the first time. I first thought he was so fake, sitting there acting like nothing happened and like we were cool when we were far from that.

Looking at him irritated me; he looked like a big-ass liar to me. I played nice for a couple of hours and answered several questions. Then I remember feeling overwhelmed by the number of people, the noise, and the emotions. My mom checked on me periodically, which helped, and she and I had our dialogue which got me out of my head, but it was a lot to process in so little time. I did like my Aunt, whom I met that night, and a cousin or two, but the biological father was still on my naughty list. That night we exchanged phone numbers, and he would reach out every so often to check on me and send me money for my birthday. As some time went on, I did ask him how he could sign away his rights to his daughter and then go and raise his current wife's daughter, but I felt like he fed me a bunch of bullshit about how it was what was best for me at the time. In my eyes, dude was selfish and did what was best for him; I am still convinced of that to this day. Not even a year after meeting this man, he tried to convince me to come to California to visit him. I was disgusted by the offer. I thought it was weird and forced, and it was not for me. I have yet to visit him in California, and I don't know that I ever will. During this same time, my dad thought getting remarried would be a good idea. Not only did he get remarried, but he did not even tell us until many months later; I was livid; this was the lying stuff that I didn't like. He ended up moving approximately an hour and a half away. He decided he would raise her two kids and forget about us. It felt like my biological father situation all over again. Needless to say, I did not take it well.

That following year, in 2017, I joined the United States Army. I remember my dad writing me one letter and my biological father writing me one. I was disappointed that my dad only wrote me one letter because that was not showing enough effort to help me get through this life- changing event. My mom ensured I had multiple letters from her every time we had a mail call. A few days before my graduation, though, I was talking to my mom about how excited I was to see everyone who was coming. She mentioned that my biological father was going to be there. When she said that, I stopped everything. It was like in the movies when all you could hear was static, and everything was blurry. Instant rage took over my body in the form of heat. I was pissed. I angrily asked her who had invited him and why he felt that was okay. Of course, instead of checking with me, he went behind my back, as always and asked my "yes," saying mother. I was furious. I was furious for multiple reasons; for one, he could have asked me himself, I am not a child, and he does not need to go to my mom about things that pertain to me. Number two, my mom should have consulted me before she just blurted out, "YES." Lastly, this man is no one to me, so why would I want him to be a part of my big moment? I didn't. I was happy that I had a few days to process it, so I reacted better when I saw him. I tried to keep the conversation to a minimum and enjoy the little time I had with my actual family. I do have to give my dad credit because he did not seem uncomfortable or irritated by this man, which I could respect.

Over the six years between then and now, we have had occasional conversations, and I invited him to things, like when I graduated from college and got married. I ask him as a friend, I address him more so as a friend, and I have expressed to him that that is where he has to start. I still do not fully understand why I invite him or what I want to get out of it, but I am still searching for that answer. In that same breath, he does not get special treatment; for example, my husband asked my dad to marry me, and my dad was the one to walk me down the aisle, not my biological father. This experience has affected me negatively and positively. It was hard on my relationship in the beginning because even though my then-boyfriend never gave me a reason to think he was cheating, I always thought he was and that he was going to just up and leave me like both of my fathers did. I always felt I was worthy of love but would never acquire it. I had a lot of anger built up in me for both my dad and my biological father that was coming out in different ways on different people, but slowly but surely, I have been chipping away at that. It also affected my relationship because I always saw my strong and independent mother. I knew my mom did not need a man, so I felt like I didn't either. I have learned that even though I don't need just any man, I do need my husband, and I want my husband, so I have to treat him accordingly. When you think of something as a want, you treat it like it is expendable, but that's not my husband; that man is not going anywhere unless we go together. That has been the hardest lesson I have learned in the quickest amount of time.

This experience has also affected me positively because it taught me a lot about myself and my strength; it has made me appreciate my dad and everything he has done for me and love my mom more than I ever thought I could. Even after all of these years, I still don't see my biological father and I ever having a father-and-daughter relationship. Today, I don't feel that for him and I am okay with it. Honestly, I think he is okay with that as well. I understand and respect that my mom wants me to have a relationship with him, but I feel he messed that up long ago.

Being pregnant now with a son and creating my own family makes me love my dad more and appreciate his presence in my life as my father. It makes me so excited to see him as a PaPa to my baby boy and I cannot wait until my son can have some of those same fishing memories that I have with my dad. Unfortunately, it also makes me dislike my biological father more. As I grow this child in my body and my husband supports and cares for me in every moment, I cannot fathom giving my baby away for any reason. I can't see myself allowing anyone else to be able to say they found and reached out to my baby even before I did. This man has never put in the effort it takes to be a father or to have a meaningful relationship with me. I refuse to do it for him as everyone else has done through this entire journey. With that, I am very happy with where I am now, physically and emotionally. I am happy with my relationship with my husband, my mother, my dad, as well as my father, and I would not have wanted my story to be any different.

FOOD FOR THOUGHT

Every choice you make has consequences. The question is, can you live with those consequences?

_____

_____

_____

_____

_____

_____

_____

_____

_____

_____

_____

_____

_____

_____

_____

_____

_____

_____

Chapter 10

MY YOUNGER SELF

What would I tell my younger self now that I'm 54? Self, everything that you're going through is all for your good. You're not going to understand or agree with that, but you must ride it out. When you think about the pain you're experiencing in relationships, friendships, and work-ships, each thing will prepare you for something else. So, always hold your head up high and have no regrets.

Assess yourself, and be honest about who you are, make the necessary changes within you to become who you want to be. Don't allow others to determine your fate or how you should live your life. Look at life as half full; what you speak out loud determines your destiny, so that means that you decide which direction your life will go. Remove all negative things and people from your inner circle.

Are you a leader? Do you want to be a leader? If you are a natural-born leader, accept and use that talent to motivate and inspire others. If it's not natural and you want to be a leader, become one by first researching those leaders that you want to emulate. Also, learn what not to do from poor leadership. Great leaders can also follow; just be mindful of who you're following. Always use your talents in a positive way and continue to let others see you through your action that corresponds with your words.

Even though you can't choose every situation in your life, you can choose how you respond. You get to decide how you handle situations that are out of your control.

Get up daily, lean on God, and watch the changes in your life.

Every decision that you make is the right decision at that time. Every time you do something, you will learn something. Give yourself a break. Know that nothing is perfect, not your body, mind, soul, or heart. Sometimes, I want you to just laugh at yourself and learn to enjoy the journey. Most of us want to plan every moment of every day, every week, and every year. Life doesn't work that way. Don't get me wrong; we must make plans and set goals. Don't let it consume you, and don't be so hard on yourself when your dreams don't go how you want them to! Look at life like every decision is a left turn and continue making left turns to add different experiences to your journey.

FOOD FOR THOUGHT

Should I tell you anything that might change some of your experiences? Would you still be you if you had all the facts early in life?

_____

_____

_____

_____

_____

_____

_____

_____

_____

_____

_____

_____

_____

_____

_____

Chapter 11

WHOSE PROTECTING YOU

Writing this book was brutal. It made me look at myself and why I might have made so many of my decisions. I may not be a God-fearing woman who can read off scriptures for every situation, but I love and am loved by my creator, which is terrific. He protected me during my career as a police officer. He carried me through the ranks to become an assistant chief at a large metropolitan agency. It wasn't easy working in a white male-dominated field. I had to pull from the strength of God many times to continue over 25 years with the department and over 30 years in law enforcement. I had children, married, and had another child during that time. I thank God my children had a dependable and present father/stepfather even though we divorced after 13 years of marriage.

Many years later, I found love again; Ken and I dated on and off for many years. I was very impatient and wanted things to happen immediately. I was reminded that life doesn't always work that way. While doing God's work on the mission field in early 2020, I asked the Lord to send me my husband; I was ready, and he responded, which surprised me, with, "I sent him to you twice, and you threw him away." I didn't believe or understand what I heard, so I asked again, and I heard the exact message "I sent him to you twice, and you threw him away." First, I wondered what he meant, and I remembered that Ken and I had broken up twice, and we were currently apart yet still friends. I was so excited; when I returned home, I couldn't wait to tell Ken. Ken smiled and said in the nicest voice; I can't tell you what you heard or that it's not true, but I'm not in that space right now; I like my life the way it is with no commitments. I care about you deeply, and you will always have a place in my heart, but I don't want to hurt you. I thought if I hung around him long enough, he would realize and be ready to move to marriage. To my surprise, that didn't happen, so I moved on to date other people, as did he. We always kept in touch; there was an unbreakable bond between us. In mid-2021, we started talking and hanging out more; feelings began to get stronger, and by early 2022 we were back together and got married on July 9, 2022. My point is this, don't give up on God; when he promises you something, he will provide.

Love yourself. I have to say that again. LOVE YOURSELF. Don't let anybody take loving yourself away from you. And remember, God loves you too. Be blessed.

FOOD FOR THOUGHT

If God blesses us with things that were not ready for, we won't succeed. But if we are patient and allow God's timing, things will work out for our good.

_____

_____

_____

_____

_____

_____

_____

_____

_____

_____

_____

_____

_____

_____

_____

_____

_____

Chapter 12

PRAY THIS PRAYER WITH ME

Everything attached to me Wins!!! Everything I put my hands to prosper! And every that rises against me in judgment, according to Isaiah chapter 54, verse 17, God will condemn! So I approach this day believing that "no weapon formed against me shall prosper!" ....in Jesus" Name! I set myself in agreement with The word, and with The Blood of Jesus, and I Cast off fear, guilt, and shame! I remind myself that The Blood was enough, I remind myself that "Jesus paid it all," ....and I restart the process of pressing towards the mark. I choose to have selective amnesia, to forget those things that are behind me, and to ask for Your Help Holy Spirit, to bring to my remembrance everything that you have spoken and everything that you've promised to do! I thank you for my past…, and I praise you for not wasting any good and bad days! Thank you for turning my "mess" into my message, and thank You, Holy Spirit, for using everything I did and everything they did to me to build Your Case for Mercy and Love. Thank you now that every day was useful…and that everything was working together for my good! I boldly declare that either way, I CANNOT lose! I CAN NOT lose! I CAN NOT lose because the season won't allow it! I CAN NOT lose because you have already won the victory…and secured my future! This is my winning season, and I decree and declare that everything attached to me wins! I'm on the winning side, and I have the victory in the name of Jesus! Victory is mine! Victory TODAY…is mine! Now be glorified in my life! Be pleased and be praised by my story! And I will forever bless Your name...it's in Jesus' Name, I pray. Amen, Amen, Amen. (Author unknown)

FOOD FOR THOUGHT

Faith of a mustard seed. How much do you have?

_____

_____

_____

_____

_____

_____

_____

_____

_____

_____

_____

_____

_____

_____

_____

_____

_____

_____

_____

_____

_____

Conclusion

Thank you again for reading this book!

I hope this book was able to help you to navigate through some harsh times and know your strength. Every experience adds to your journey. Shift, pivot, and turn until you travel the road you want.

Finally, if you enjoyed this book, please take the time to share your thoughts and post a review. I would greatly appreciate it!

Thank you!

About Author

Sonya Hudson is a retired Assistant Chief of the DeKalb County Police Department. She served her community as a law enforcement professional for over 30 years. Sonya served her country as a Corporal in the United States Marine Corps for 4 years; she has taken her military and Law enforcement training in leadership and translated it into pursuing her passion for helping people live their best lives.

Sonya holds a Bachelor's degree in Criminal Justice from Saint Leo University and a Master of Science degree in Public Administration from Troy University. She is an entrepreneur and co-owns two thriving businesses, T & T Bakery and The Rose@BayRose. In addition, Sonya is a Certified Professional Life Coach specializing in leadership.

Sonya is the proud wife of Kenneth Hudson, mother of Tamika, Tamia, son-in-law Kenny, Michael, and bonus son, Jordan. Tyler, her grandson, is the light of her life. She is a local and global missionary serving in Belize, South Africa, Costa Rica, Central America, and the United States. When not on the mission field or spending time with family, Sonya loves empowering young adults as a basketball coach.

* 9 7 8 1 9 5 3 7 6 0 1 6 6 *